CITRUS FASHION

Collected Poetry

Brandon Hale

Dorrance Publishing Co
585 Alpha Drive
Suite 103
Pittsburgh, PA 15238
Visit our website at *www.dorrancebookstore.com*

ISBN: 979-8-8860-4418-8
eISBN: 979-8-8868-3839-8

Oranges, Limes, & Lemons

The trees and bushes bear colorful fruit

Summer's glow illuminates the minute

Plans of good times permeate the hot air

Backyards fences hide the lounging of lawn chairs

Each moment of this solstice

Eternal in its joys

Regardless of fleeting youth and its lack of poise

The concentrated juice,

Pulled up from the roots

Could fill a glass refreshing and tall

Let this feeling last forever

Lest life make gardeners of us all

Sunseeker

Saw your car at the station this morning

Knew what was coming when you said this town was boring

You like fast living

When life gets slow

But when the change rushes in too wild

You're afraid to let go

No need to explain it away,

I'm on that highway too

I know what that's like

Hollow that your past keeps you glued to

You've shut the door now,

Filled up your tank,

Saw that wide smile as you drove off,

Like taking a check to the bank

And I'd never say this out loud

But I'm glad we didn't talk

Because when life didn't give me what I wanted

I never had the courage to walk

Seagulls

The golden sky beams upon the sand where I stand

Ocean water faintly grazing my tired ankles

I take a rest to bask in the sensation

But it does not seep beyond my skin

The sunlight does not project its warmth on my heart

The wind fails to stir my wonder

And no matter how encompassing,

The sea cannot reach my soul

I am bound to the ground

Planted in this world

I sit and watch the seagulls

As they glide and dive

Free as grains in the breeze

And for but a moment,

I wish I were among them

Zippo

Here he comes

Crossroad smile

Presence that could part the meek and the mild

Jet black car

Fresh paint job

Dark as char

King of the bar,

He lights up one

Flicks open his chrome

Flame hits the tip

Now he's home

The beer, a reprieve

These lies that we weave

The sadness, a sickness

Waiting for vigor to cleave

Half-past four

Ashes hit the floor

Remarks about youth,

An unhappy truth

Last glasses of vermouth

Have the best days passed you by?

Are you just another drunk in the sea of night flies?

Things to ponder as he looks up at the sky

He once called a ceiling

Now these confines provide too comfortable a feeling

Cigarette

The bar lights dim and the room begins to clear

Closing time

"See ya, Jim!" the bartender chimes

Jim mumbles something mundane

Exiting into the city streets as he had the night prior

A cigarette is pulled from his right pocket,

Then a lighter from his left

The smoke wraps around,

Shrouds him

Blocking this foreign world

A small semblance of comfortability

Memories and dreams long lost cross the trodden pathways of his mind

He entertains all the possibilities

What might have been

These daydreams wound

But they also comfort

The virtue of imagination is a stretched hand

One he cannot let go of

Not another living soul is observed

There are no hearts around to feel him

No ears to hear him

Not a sound

Save the deafening cacophony of the mind

The smoke has faded

The light is out

Jim stands at the entrance to his apartment complex

Resigned to be an alien,

Waiting to be human again

Pier

Saw you striding up the pier

Pushing papers

Worshiping beer

Just when you think you're in the clear,

Friends will shock you

Show you a mirror

Evenings

When the sun hangs down

The sky turns orange

Lights flicker on

And workers go home

I watch the cars pass me by

Chasing some phantom destination down the street

I peer through the picture window

Standing at ground level with all the rest

I touch my hands to the glass and hope for a better tomorrow

Maybe someday I will know what I wish for

Victims of Billboards

"First time in LA?"

I heard the train driver say

Praying and nodding through my reply

"I just hope it works out my way"

Railcar doors melt away

Stepping into the arid day

Warming my skin

The whole thing just makes your head spin

Taking in this fabled land

A shining monument to brand

I can see those pretty women playing games in the sand

I feel the cool grip of death in my shaking hand

Walking along the shoreside

Losing track of time

I can feel my pulse quicken

As I exit my prime

Tennis Court

A crisp spring day

Upon the cusp of summer

Where the tennis players lay

Garbed in white and other brilliant colors

Soaking sun and red wine, shirts unstained

On their crescent hilltop

Further lust for gluttony unchained

So far removed from labor bodies and sweatshops

Feeding each craving

Yet they flash an image of justice

Drawing crowds with pandering ravings

A hushed mockery of the populace

Their voices are like razors

Dulled with cool words

They can manufacture life

They can create new worlds

Long Beach Kids

Skateboard wheels grind up against the pavement

Powerful and evocative

Momentum carries meaning

A truth foreign to some

Kids clad in off-season clothes give this gauntlet a run

Words wrapped in phony irony

Sarcasm drenched

Live and die by things decried

A lust for purpose unquenched

Crimewave

Wicked fire envelops the rooftops

Midnight glass falls to the ground

The shattered dreams of the city's poor

cloud the sidewalk

Never making a sound

The tension is as palpable

as the heat of an overcrowded street,

Those happy news crews rush in again,

Salivating like a sick dog to a treat,

And at the end of it all,

A politician stands on the concrete

He mumbles something about relief

Followed shortly by a fearful retreat

Statistics

Through those browned blinds

I can see the end rise

The great weight that ties

Escapism for you and me

Skewed our destiny in ways we could not see

Our love is like a gentle rain

Waning softly as we wash down the pain

Needles and bottles

They came on just too quick

Reprieve and relief with just a small prick

Shying away when they called us "addict"

A label I would rebuff with words emphatic

It was all just through the same motions

Time and time again

'Till I rode down to city hall,

I could see it all

Realization bearing down like an oppressive wall

Those freaks and junkies

Objects of ire

Had too become slaves to substance we desire

I wish it were easy

Easy to flee

Yet the chains that bind make us feel free

And I wish I could say that it was too late for me

Yet it was you who paid the price

Skin draining of color,

Cold as ice

A wretched result

The pursuit of some high

We should have found in one another's eye

Your flower is wilting away

Floating on an uneasy breeze

I will sit so still by your pedals

And give your hands a desperate squeeze

Order

Intrigue sparks a fire impossible to quell

Soon you'll find out the world you thought you knew so well,

Well, you don't know it from an icicle in hell

Soon everything you know is engulfed in a blaze

Questioning is chaos

Who will bring the order to this maze?

The young girls longing for change?

The silver can sipping everyman who couldn't care less?

The CEOs on the hunt for virtuous green,

Mangling all the rest?

Sifting through the slideshow, you find nothing acceptable

TV puppets and their string fiddlers,

Icons of the week,

Poets and authors,

Everyone has the answer

Until the clock strikes 13

Sweet & Sour

Sweet and sour all the way down

Sour comes on too strong,

Stays a little too long

Sweet delights are such a treat

Yet move with haste to retreat

As with meat in heat

I can feel the earth spoil beneath my feet

The chaff overtaking the wheat

Clouds overtake the sky rapidly

Battling the sunshine like an Imperial fleet

Roy

Roy is a strange boy

He reminisces on a past that he didn't belong to

He dreams of a future that will not come to pass

He is adrift

Caught between here and now

Latching onto anything that lasts

But he doesn't beg for stillness

He only wishes to steer the mast

Melancholia

Nowhere to go

Who will you be?

Once you stop running,

Running from me?

I'll live in your soul

When you're left behind

When the clouds loom

Dark and unkind

Life's changing winds roar and whip

I'll still be here

No moment left untainted

By my exposing leer

Renewing sun stolen

And that's just the thing

You're defined by melancholy

Snuggly trapped,

Beneath the curve of my wings

Unmasked

Cold

Crisp nothingness in the air

Sunlight is dulled

The world's exterior is acid washed, it's interior rotten

A walk to the shore becomes a test of fortitude

Wonder

Wonder where all the color has gone

Wonder if you can outrun your mind

Ask if this is it

No reply

Warrior

Sword, serrated steel

Warriors clashing endlessly

There are no victors, no victims

A battlefield upon the plain of one's mind

They never rest

Even while the world around them lies at peace

The struggle to overcome oneself consumes all

And vanquishes

The Ascent

Wisdom is like standing on a mountain top

You think silently at the foot of the slope

Heavy snow falls around

Blanketing a bone-gnawing cloud

Before the ascent has even begun

Spirits fall,

Good times may fade,

And bad times may linger

Like the stain of accusation upon a pointed finger

Heat is so cherished on days of cool reflection

Yet the winter will leave a permanent mark

And the scent of liquor mars its spark

Stark,

The contrast between yesterday and today

This climb, its incline

Being trekked in large numbers

With the sky a solemn gray

Some walked

Others picked up the pace and flew

They tell you of warmth

But they're just as cold as you

Teenage Wanderer

A crisp burning scent singes your nostrils

You laugh and say to pass it forward

Calm

Mysticism

Curiosity

The fragmented souls that scatter the room become one

Like opulent metals to a bartering table

You cling to the worn couch

A barrel of smiles clicks a TV remote

A mellow heart adds music

Wondrous soundwaves

An engrossing video

The barrage of sensations flows through you like a wave into the

beach's sands

And just for this brief flash,

We are platinum

Still Going

Three unlikely wanderers blaze forward

The curse of circumstance binding them no longer

Summer heat rips through the tree line like a knife to butter

Bringing life to nature

Blessing the emerald grass with vibrant color

Everything halts as new dawn is reached,

Entering the mouth of the trail

They meld into the earth's palette

Socialite

Strangers with familiar faces float along

Hypnotized by the sounds of a late Friday night

School's been let out

Parents just out of sight

There's a crowd gathering,

Gawking while two drunkards fight

I had thought coming here would make me feel whole

Now my emptiness runs deeper than ever

Just like a machine that runs on coal

Imagination is obsolete, unable to weather

I smoke & drink, laugh & lust

I blend in to a fault

Because it's all I can trust

Old perspectives fade away, oxidize, and rust

A rowdy band plays a teenage psalm

Who knew our wild passions could be so wrong?

Our communal faults bring comfort and calm

Somewhere in the back,

Where the music fades out,

A girl parades in a vivacious blaze,

She's everything a boy could dream about

I claw courage from the ground,

Hot like molten rock

As lines are rehearsed in my head

As I unknowingly run the clock

"Your eyes shine like a gem"

"Take me for a dance"

"In this age of loneliness,

Would you be my one last chance?"

Trapped in my contemplative haze,

The girl brushes past

Out of sight and into the crowd

My confidence fading fast

I wouldn't tell my friends,

I'd just be another joke to them

In my stupor, I dart around

Overwhelmed by mental phlegm

A rest is taken

And I look in the mirror

Wondering when I'll understand what's missing

Paralyzed by fear

My thoughts are interrupted by a striding triad,

The one in the middle says "Cheer up kid, it's a party

be glad!"

Last Call

I don't care what your college plans are,

I don't mind that you barely know my name,

I'm not too sure what I'm looking for,

'Cause I'm tired of playing this game,

Youth is fading away,

Like a cracked hourglass,

While we were trapped in small time conversation,

An hour came and passed,

I missed the train to academia,

Then was berated by the media,

The walk back would've been fine,

Were it not for the men at the library,

All standing in a lengthy line,

The brown blazer had something to say,

He stood on the stairs and let his thoughts run away,

"There's a guy that's walking free!"

I pepped up my step, taking his words with glee,

Took me ages to realize they weren't talking to me,

What is my place without a degree?

Monte Carlo

The Clatter of pins subside as I follow him out,

He takes a slow drag off his fixed nail,

Chaining him to this moment,

Thankful for the pause,

I stand quietly beside him,

Waiting for some seed of conversation to plant itself within our minds,

I want to say all that needs to be said,

Before you've retreated back into your head,

Before my fervor dissipates and my emotions have shed,

You mean the world to me,

Do I mean the world to you?

You can spout it all day,

But it won't make it true,

I know you're trying your hardest,

I am too,

But how can I grow my wings without learning how you flew?

You're my father,

You're my hero,

But it would be a grotesque lie,

To say I don't think about the two of us

And release a longing sigh

Window Shopping

White knuckles on the steering wheel,

Warm night air in my hair,

What better way to start this new beginning

Than a long rearview glare?

What fresh sorrows will my soul have to bear?

How many mountains must I move to make you care?

It seems like I'm always running,

Looking for something I can't find,

Then when I'm gone,

I'll string myself along,

And wonder about those I've left behind,

Whether it be a new city, state, or town,

I'll arrive with the same baggage in tow,

Hoping it'll get lost somewhere under a faint neon glow,

Yet, the past is my ball and chain,

Its mistakes are my crown,

Which I flaunt all too proudly,

Like a young lover's wedding gown,

I search for signs of life on this late interstate,

I can't find it in the passing headlights,

And certainly not on my license plate

Once In a Lifetime

High Tops touch the stone walkways,

Passing cheap thrill games

Water guns

Clowns

Lights strung up, blinking along the path

Flurries of blurry red, blue, green

The young couple enters a train car

Soaring high into the air

They feel the wind hit their face

Their hands clasp the cold guard rail, brushing against each other

Full stop

Just like that

The ride ends

As they look into each other's eyes, they know

The attraction is just beginning

Treading Water

Somewhere at the edge of what is and what was

We sit fixed on a knife's edge

Clinging onto each other

Petrified to fall off the ledge

Our arms get tired,

Knees grow weak

But no, I won't let go

Not while the faint light still glows

Not while my heart still beats

Eyes Like Dreams

Peer through this glass I'm peering through,

There is many a sight to see, but all I see is you,

Wonder how much of my vision is true,

The curiosity in my heart is tangible and bright

Let our souls conjoin and fill me with delight

City Flowers

I can recall mellow clouds

Pale lilac and purple shrouds

As Evening falls, Autumn rises

And your memory springs to mind

Somewhere deep in my delusions

I picture our city apartment

Before your reflection became too much to bear

You wore a mirror in your eyes

And I hated that stare

We'd both wear berets,

Pretend we're artists,

We'd strum the air enthusiastically,

Sing choruses like a banshee,

Mimicking our cherished records

While we watched dull TV

But I just couldn't see

The world wasn't a playground

And we weren't those same kids we used to be

We grew directionless

Grew too comfortable

Grew an unhealthy confidence in what we called usual,

So when we grew apart, it seemed all too natural

An unfortunate consequence of a love so organic

We became cynical,

Twisted what we had into something so clinical,

Midnight movie marathons became late-night shifts,

And those dull tv episodes became all-too-exciting gifts

The purple flower by the windowsill wilted,

So I stumbled past the florist and bought two

One a deep red

One a sickly blue,

Now sitting alone on this ragged couch built for two,

I catch your scent still lingering in the dead air,

An unwanted sensation that drags me back,

Tears flow as I picture purple shrouds,

And that pale lilac...

The Velvet Spire

We say the love will last forever

That we shall die in each other's arms

An eternity left to fall again and again

For those soothing charms

That staircase we climb

Fragrant with roses and thyme

Yet we forget time

It's erosion,

It's perversions,

It's grime,

Before we have reached that perch

One of us will say goodbye

The other will ask the whys,

Grow bitter over those classic lines

Descending those steps we used to tread together

We'll pass each other along the way

Melancholic at this gloomy weather

I'll saunter blindly ahead

Wondering about things left unsaid

Years go by

And the tides will change

Old scents of love will be replaced by sage

As you ascend again someday, with another man in toe

I will extend a friendly hand

And we shall let a new understanding flow

Perimeter Stroll

The horizon city lights shine bright tonight

Railroading my mind into visions of flight

Wielding within me some intrepid might

Colors of brown, blue, orange, and white

The land and the skyline fuse in height

I can see the stars traveling

Filling my eyes with a blinding light

Legacy

Solemnly looking at the gravestone

Damp with April rain

And again I find myself in quiet anger

Placing the flowers and picture frame

All that you were

Reduced to a name

Chiseled into flat gray rock

A creative spirit they couldn't tame,

A fiery temper that had accumulated great fame

I was curious if you were truly at rest

'Cause the winds have come to carry me west

With feelings of fulfillment and dread

Your words running roughshod throughout my head

I question my own motives

Laying in the shade you made

Shall I repeat your mistakes

Or let your memory fade?

Roadside Light

That dim streetlamp flickers

Casting rays on the slick roadway

I thought it mimicked my breath

Panicked and self-assuring

Circumstances disconcerting

Years on the express

Few things have stayed constant

I cling to these remaining factors

The roots amidst the wind

Yet the route I carve out with a flurry of forward steps

Has torn the ground,

Split the grass

My heart remains on those wooden railcar tracks

The apex of my past

To truly greet the morning sun

This mournful nostalgia cannot last

Blue Jay Day

"Don't live in a dull way!"

Says the Blue Jay,

Her sentiments harden me,

Mold me like clay,

She flies on by,

She comforts my sky,

She tells me of the beauty,

The beauty in my eyes

When I see her brilliant blue,

Shimmering in that hot summer sunrise,

I am thankful for an angel,

An angel so wise

Golden Gaze

You're my world,

My Earth,

My stars,

My Moon,

When the dawn breaks you bring me drops of June

So fair,

So kind,

Our hearts combined,

Woven like a warm winter sweater

Fixed upon my mind

Vanilla Milkshake

A cherry red car pulls off the highway

I sip my empty milkshake in soft envy

The waitress's aviators slip down her nose

Vibrant colors move us

Citrus fashion

Flashy clothes

Sun bright Chevy

Only costs a penny

Just one thought, and I can start a new day

Now I'm back to the asphalt

Radio pops on

A loud rock tune

I look behind me as it fades so fast

I'll drive ahead, grab the future while it lasts

And I'll keep on smiling; it's sunny in June

Nothing ties me down

I leave behind Earth's salt

Traveling into the dune

Afternoon Streets

The rain clouds have parted

Like a road splits in two

Down the highway, through and through

He's just about done being blue

His hands reach far above his head

To touch the soft, warm hue

Long after hours, he walks back home

Far, far away from the streets of Rome

Splashing color along the way

He's grabbed a piece of the sky today

And he'll hold onto it

long after his world fades back to gray

On The Town

Take me out tonight,

Take me out on the town!

By the end of this young light,

You won't be wearing a frown,

From our shared laughter,

I'll fashion a crown,

Youthful love borders art,

You are the queen of my soul,

You are the owner of my heart

A Starlight Love

Sometimes I lament how fast life seems to change,

The new dawns and sunsets can be a bit strange,

But no matter what fades,

What new problems manifest,

You still make me feel a love so strong,

Deep within my chest,

Looking your best,

So flawless,

So effortless,

Your passion and compassion,

Shocking me in a sense,

With your delicate touch,

Comfort is always within range,

You're my guiding star,

And a starlight love we'll exchange

A Cambrian Evening

I can see you there,

Your sky pale face,

Your silky auburn curls gently waving in the breeze,

The tall spruce shielding us from the sun's gaze,

The college lawn,

The faint scent of falling night draws me back to a simpler time,

I struggle to find my words,

You calmly grasp my wrist with a sweet smile,

"Get your pen; write before the thought is gone."

Seasons of the Mind

Exhaust and ache

With this song and dance

They pull me in,

Push me away,

I yearn to leave,

Yet cling to stay

Fires of circumstance harden my clay,

Maybe on a sunny day, far away

I'll chip the layer with chimes of may

Seasons of the Mind II

Wanting nothing but success and a smile,

Hampering myself along the way,

Never achieving now

Never trying later,

The absence of progress leaves a considerable crater

May the faint heat that thaws these hands persevere

Many aspects of my soul are still left to shear

Pictures of a Modern Sky

The masquerading poet has fooled himself at last,

Thinking he has seen beyond the thin veneer

An outer crust where a core is pictured,

He sees gray clouds

Brick buildings

Waving flags

Desperate youth in a cold environment,

Shades of red and blue fading backward,

Quasi depression,

No drive or motivation,

Yet sunlight still peaks through the hall,

Reflecting off the cars as they rush onto the streets,

Voices shrilling with optimism

And recoiling in horror,

Fence-sitters stain the last white pickets

Even further removed,

The poet sits in his room,

Studying himself in the mirror

This, just like that spinning globe around him,

He feigns to understand,

There is a better world somewhere,

Even if only in his head,

A classic dreamer true to the word,

You'll find him dreaming alone on his hot nail bed,

A vision of his own design,

Maybe he'd even bother to achieve it,

"If only he'd had the time"

Tandy's Song

Tandy the trumpeter sits on the boardwalk,

Orange Sun burning low,

He makes his trumpet cry as the daylight fades to nighttime,

The kids stride back and forth under cheap neon lights,

Gracing their ears with his subtle warmth and his jazzy hue,

Nobody stops,

His tone fades to the weather,

His horn bleeds into the wind,

In days long past, he was the #1 act,

Even got some girls, as a matter of fact,

But the past is sand through our hands,

And he was just another grain trying to battle the marching breeze,

Now he's on a small-town coast,

Somewhere acquainted with the palm trees,

His feelings are so hard to express,

So far from the city, he once called his home,

Now he's just stuck where the others roam,

Shades of blue on his broken throne,

The folks, locals, and passers-by don't mind him much,

They say he adds to the small-town charm,

But he rejects this background label,

Because he is a human being,

Not an evening alarm,

Through his soft suites,

He mutters about a world that has forgotten him,

He wonders about the old clubs, The big hair, dive bars, and those

fancy cars,

How long's it been since he's seen a fancy car?

The sun's going down, and there's pastel in the sky

Tandy's packing up, and a boy passes by

He says, "I love your playing, mister!

You make my day and night;

You raise up my soul

And you mellow out my fright,

I'm a huge fan of yours,

You just don't see,

The passionate fire you've lit inside of me,

I've got the rhythm in me now

And that rhythm makes me feel so free!"

The trumpeter tears up,

Silent for a moment in that revealing, howling moonlight,

Tandy pats the teen on his shoulder,

They can feel the beat between them

 and that's a strong connection,

Good Ol' T turns the other direction,

"Thank you for your joy; it's been so long since I've seen a real smile,

You seem like a bright young man,

I hope you stick around this town awhile."

As he walks away, he tries not to look back,

Lest he reconnect with his youth, buried in that foreign ash,

Tandy faintly hopes to play again tomorrow,

But his enthusiasm is long gone,

He can hear his friend's big band playing symphonies up in the

dark sky now,

And he knows it won't be long

Til' he's played his last swing song

The Clock & The Watchmaker

The watchmaker sits back and admires his craft,

Sterling silver with a black leather band,

The world is pulled into a spiral around the face's hands,

Trading pieces of his life

To make wrist clocks,

Yet his time never came,

The people never stopped

Left with the awful ticking,

Products of his labor

The horrific drumming march of the second hand

Chiming away in his ear

Hours,

Days,

Years float on by without so much as a sigh,

There is only life sucked and wasted,

Only the clock and the watchmaker

Harry's Last Waltz

Damn that rising sun

Harry hated mornings,

Always had,

Yet at this strange hour

He springs out of bed

Silently jolly,

Hopeful that the night's dance

Will bring an end to things,

One final folly

This daylight is a slide he rides

The prospect of punctuation chips his blues,

Cracks his frown,

Breaking him into newfound strides

Each calendar strike prior

Was nothing but ailing hills

Falling and crashing

Pushing him down to this disparaged mire

Long had he waited,

The moment would soon be here,

Starlight fell on his little town,

His surroundings now in the clear

"These dancing shoes fit perfectly!"

 Harry's mind exclaims

He steps upon the beggar's chair

Icey death now fixed in his gaze

The ballroom doors swing open

The dead man grabs his hand

The first step of the waltz begins

No longer present for Earth's demands

The bastion is pushed aside

Legs now in free fall

The second step of his final dance,

His chair slams against the wall

The lights go dim

Everything fades

Harry's last waltz

Die like a craze

Welcome Home Marine

The sound of beer bottles clinking

The liquid shrinking

Shoes tapping on the tavern ground

With floorboards shrieking

Just your first night back at the local bar

And what could be more swell than your brand-new sports car?

But something's not quite right

It doesn't feel the same

This music is far too vapid

And your heart can't take the shame

The girls greet you as a hometown hero

They cling to your arm

But you just smile sheepishly

Because you know of the harm

The mind keeps falling back

A sudden heart attack

With gunfire screaming out they say

"Nice Shot, Mac"

That was when you killed your first man

Just an 18-year-old boy

They put a rifle in your hand

Feet planted on American soil

But your mind in the desert sand

This noise is much too loud

And you don't wanna cry, no,

Not in front of this happy crowd,

You're far too proud

Never forgetting the faces,

All your friends from the platoon

Too many have died

And oh how they lied

When they sold the "Thrills" and "Adventure"

For now,

It's the town streets you'll once again roam

Except there's no place to hide and nowhere that feels like home

Too many bitter pills,

Too many to chew

So now you toss and turn at night

Thinking that it should have been you

Another walk in solitude

You see a banner strewn

Just more decor for this urban machine

In a utilitarian font it says:

"Welcome Home, Marine!"

Palm Tree Blues

Palm tree blues,

Must I shift this green Earth,

Just to lace my brown shoes?

Red hot anger mocks the yellow sun,

Heat blankets the greyed pavement,

Choking my steps one-by-one,

Composure stays hidden away,

Stowed inside a darkened clamshell,

I pry it open with all my strength,

Searching like hell

Doves & Crows

You're warmth on sunkissed skin

Like California sun

Yet you leave me so cold

Like a New York blizzard run

Stay fixed in my head

Don't leave when I'm at my best

Your quick vacancy brings dread,

Weights in my chest

Oh coveted happiness

How it comes and goes,

It dives and it shows

Doves and crows

Doves and crows

About The Rain

Tapping on the window

Water streaks down the glass

Gliding like the flow of an ancient aqueduct,

Built to last

My muscles ache

My mind is relaxed

Paralyzed in some malaise

Darkness encroaches in its familiar, comfortable ways

Yet today, I grow tired of this haze

I have run out of excuses to give

No more lies left to live

Some control still rests in my hands

Unrested by the cold and its clear plans

Stepping outdoors, the droplets hit my face

Not a man to challenge me,

And a dream still left to chase

Something about the rain

Quiets my refrain

It may have stolen my smile

But it will not take my brain

Trail

Choked and exhausted

Leisurely stepping into nature

Behold refreshment and repair no man can replicate

Ash clouds made of words,

Stresses,

Fears,

Slowly wither

They die and ignite passion,

Hope

A seasoned sprint begins in no particular direction

A sigh of reprieve

I glance to the old oaks that have seen victory and pain

How lucky am I now to stand among them

The running shoes glide past the goal post,

Weightless

The Orb

You crash ashore on a distant beach

The grand voyage that tossed you here is unknown

Wet and afraid, you cling to the warmth of the sand

Maybe somewhere within, you can find the courage to stand

Fret not; you needn't look far for inspiration

A mysterious figure and a radiant orb lie engulfed in palm trees

"Looking for guidance?"

A head nods

A hand turns

The ball of white brilliance flows into an abyss

"Follow"

You don't see the orb

Yet still, you dive

Stardust

Beneath the sparkling starlight that has witnessed all, I was reborn

Baptized in waters of life

Shipped downriver to a settlement of foreign nature

My soul collapsed under the weight of intrigue

My journey, void of tempest

All that embarked were conjoined

My comrades of experience moved alongside me

Through the fields of many colors

Past the animals that inhabit this place

Our guide kept us safe, led us to the heat of a crackling fire

Distrust rose until I shared a piece of nature in communion

Light envelopes us even in darkness

Even as the soundwaves sink into the soil

Alone, I found myself soaring through a sacred temple

Infinite

Domino

A tape is distorted each time it plays

Like a phase of dreary days

Same old things

In the same old ways

A chuckle for the gods

They shine down rays for our domino game

I watch them fall to the ground

What a sickening sound,

Taunting musicality

When it's thought to be over

Something unknown

Plucked anew from the toy chest they call reality

Something gained

Or something lost

I cannot assure

Only that curiosity is poised to replace azure

Sunglasses

A man sets up camp in a strange desert.

Despite the great myths he was fed,

The land sat barren

Day after day,

The sand bleached his boots

The advance of the setting sun all that drove him forward

"One more day," he says

And he says

And he says

Silk Shore

Soft sand on the shore

Warmth and glow to all who walk the beach

Billboards and shoreline that stretch past the sun

Deep blue waves cradle evening swimmers

Neon lights shimmer and coalesce with nature

May I wander life's lands for eternity

Verdant with intrigue

Jenny's Pennies

Clock in

And clock out

Day in

And day out

Jenny was a working girl,

Was a well-known fact

Windowpane factory shrouds swore she'd die of a heart attack

But the boss tossed his dollars

And the girl was still smiling

A tough week's pay,

The handsome sums she'd been riling

But soon,

Too soon enough,

She needed more

This direct path had become quite the chore

Her mother's fate, dead at forty-four

Honesty can kill if you let it

So Jenny found the edge of morality and met it

Ground floor

She became a snake oil peddler

Traveling door to door

Days of panes and oil

Grew a too familiar toil

And with the wealth of a royal

She planted her feet right there in that Louisiana soil

From seeds sprouted an empire of legend

But years of conning just brings you to the edge and,

Vision is lost of a past perspective

Friends become workers

And work is a binary directive

Who had she become?

Jenny was no detective

Things always look so good when standing on top

The lowest ladder rungs seem such a sharp drop

Those workers at the bottom fill in their little timecards

And Jenny tosses pennies that fall down like glass shards

Garden of Warmth

Oh, darling

Oh, darling

My sunflower with brilliant petals

You sit planted in a garden of wilted flowers,

Dead trees,

Yet still, you sway in the wind,

The world will cherish your radiant glow,

When you transform all around you into a garden of warmth

Sunday In Central Park

Gorgeous hazel eyes enrapture mine

All else fades to negligible noise

As I embrace those loving arms

Once again with a genuine joy

The way the sun rattles through your hair…

Honey, it sends me there

A scene that brings the wicks of artists to flare

I was a flame upon your lips in the summertime

Back then you said:

"Love is a ladder for only fools to climb"

We are all jesters in our own mind

For now, let us unwind

And unravel this tension that plagues our kind

White Horizon

A shine and a shimmer

My soul will deliver

Where once I would shiver

Now I softly simmer

Bringing forth to the broth of an untamed day

Prospects anew strengthen my resolve

And bring biting sadness to decay

Many pray,

As I have

For pastures a brilliant green

I know not yet if I've reached them

But at last, the mind is clean

Growing Down

You are eight years old,

Soaring high into the air, bouncing on a new trampoline your dad

set up last weekend

You remember a golden sun and your smile glistening

Your knee hurts

You fell off the trampoline

You're crying now

Mom and Dad are fighting on the porch by the pool

A familiar sight that makes you sad

You wish you were five again

When dad still hugged mom

When you all had picnics together on the porch

When the math tests weren't so hard

How rotten it is that you're robbed of your fun

You wish you were younger

You are 17 years old

It's your senior year of high school

You're saying goodbye to all your friends

Graduation day

"Is this the last time I'll see them?"

"Where do I go from here?"

"Will my new friends be just as great?"

"Will I make new friends?"

You hated school

But yet, you don't want to leave

You think back

Back to when you fucked around in class

Back to when you all smoked weed in your pal's basement

Back to when you had your first kiss by the pier on that summer night

How sickening it is to leave your whole world behind; you just

built it

You wish you were younger

You wish you appreciated all of those things before they slipped

from your grasp,

You are 85 years old

Bedridden

Your family surrounds the bedside

Kids and Grandkids

Your loving wife of 50 years

The doctors said that you'd pass tonight

Faces are soaked with tears

Your eldest son asks you in wispy breaths

"Do you regret anything? Do you wish you could go back?"

You think for a moment

Mustering your scarce energy

"No son, I wouldn't have had it any other way.

Peace Forever

Lush grass and ruby poppies stretch on

Seemingly endless

No inch unknown upon first viewing

The sky is a crystal sheet of glass

The sunbeams with glowing rays

Projecting no heat

The delicate scent of morning dew grass would grace you

If you could smell anything at all

A perfect wooden ranch house rests upon a hilltop

Thousands of voices breeze toward

Glancing across your delicate skin

As you ascend the slope, everything melts away

All worries

All doubts

All fears

Elation is the only emotion resulting from sight

You think for a moment

Perhaps it was never so complicated

You embrace exactly who you had been waiting to see

Finally

Peace forever

Rotten Fruit

There will come a time when your vibrance will fade

Those fond of the midday stroll will run for the shade

And those qualities so adored about yourself and your ways

They get lost in life's complexity,

Slow in its decays

Baskets of fruit,

Rich in zest

Do not stay preserved,

Forever at their best

Enjoy each sensation

These small handfuls of color

The freshness will pass

The tone may be duller

About the Author

Brandon Hale is a 19-year-old writer and college student from Lockport, New York. He began working on poems during the initial stages of the Covid-19 pandemic, primarily out of boredom. This quickly turned to excitement as he saw the potential of exploring a new creative outlet for himself. Struggles with mental health contributed to the themes in his work and continue to do so in the present day. He is also known to frequently draw inspiration from art and music.

Outside of writing, Hale enjoys running, rock and roll, hi-fi equipment, and soft drinks.